The Secret Ocean

Three musical settings of poems by Mark Jarman

for Soprano and Piano

Music by
Evan Mack

Commissioned by Amy Jarman and the Blair School of Music, Vanderbilt University, 2016

Dedicated to Danielle Mack

The first performance was given on September, 23, 2017 by soprano Amy Jarman and pianist Jennifer McGuire at Vanderbilt University's Blair School of Music.

The Children

Poem by Mark Jarman

Evan Mack

Lyrics under the vocal line:
The chil-dren are hi-ding a-mong the rasp-ber-ry canes.

4

They look big to one a - no-ther, the gar-den

small.

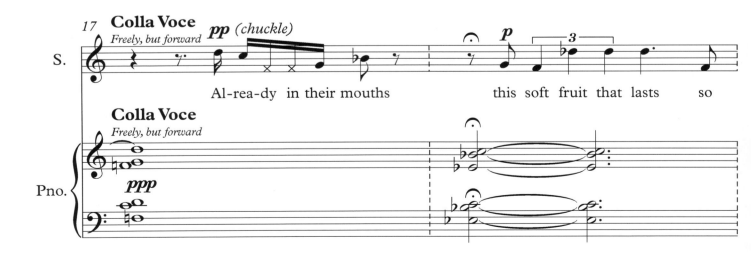

Al-rea-dy in their mouths this soft fruit that lasts so

6

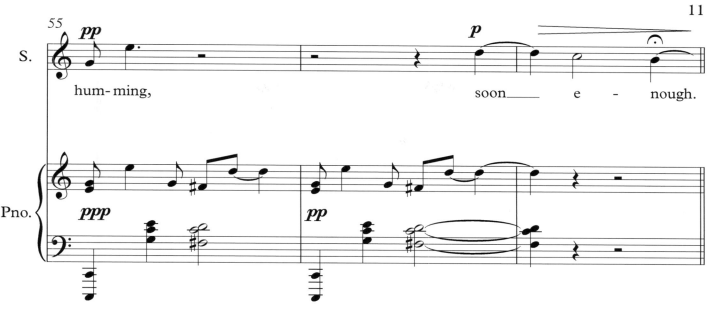

hum- ming,   soon___ e - nough.

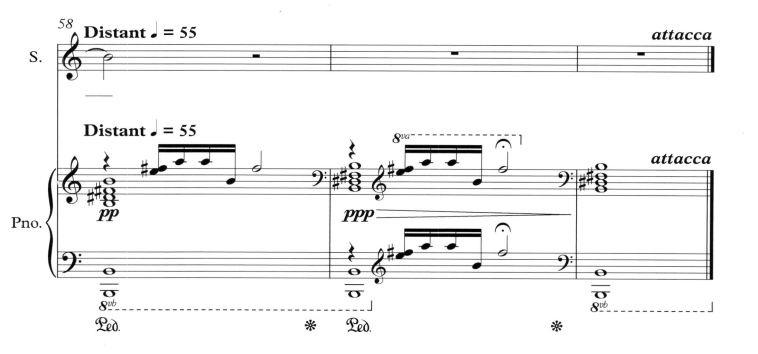

After Disappointment

feel a-lone, not know-ing_____ what you should or should - n't

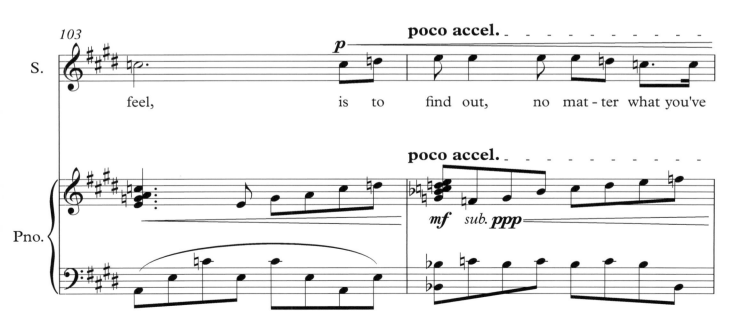

feel, is to find out, no mat - ter what you've

16

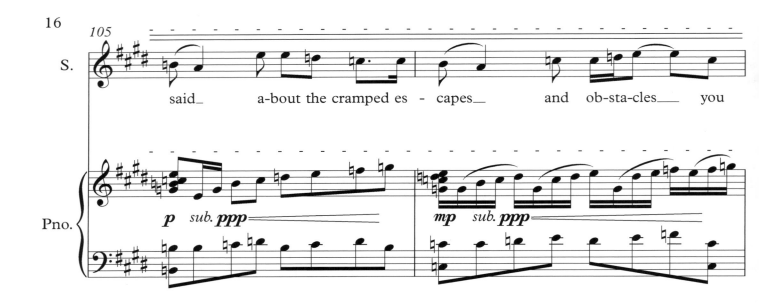

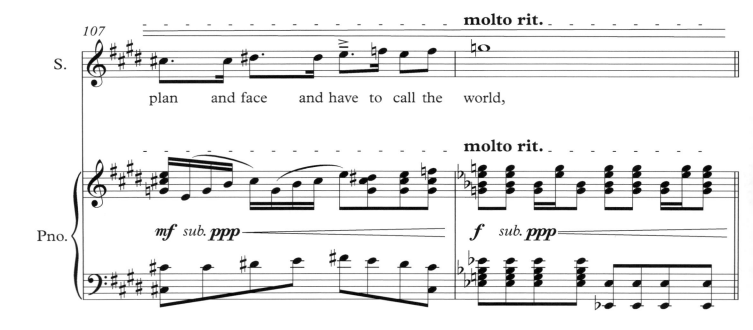

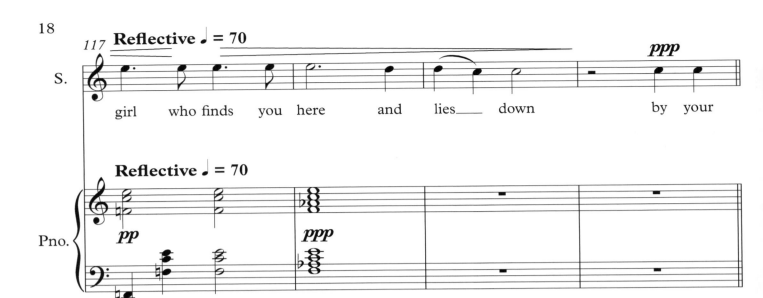

girl   who finds   you   here   and   lies____ down   by   your

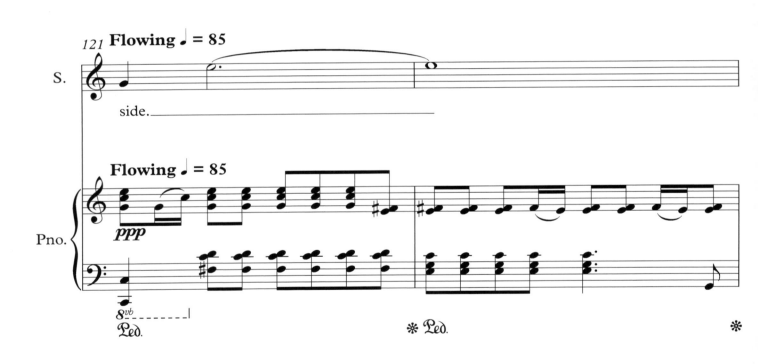

side.____

The Secret Ocean

Free, but forward ♩ = 70

When you were lit-tle girls,— I brought you here to light weav-ing on wa-ter—— a-mong trees, with one of you be-side me, walk-ing a-long, the o-ther on my shoul-ders, talk-ing to her-self.—— We found this

20

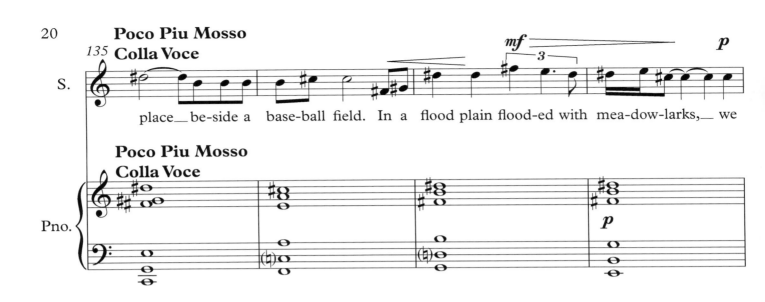

and the air._____ A wa - ter strid - er

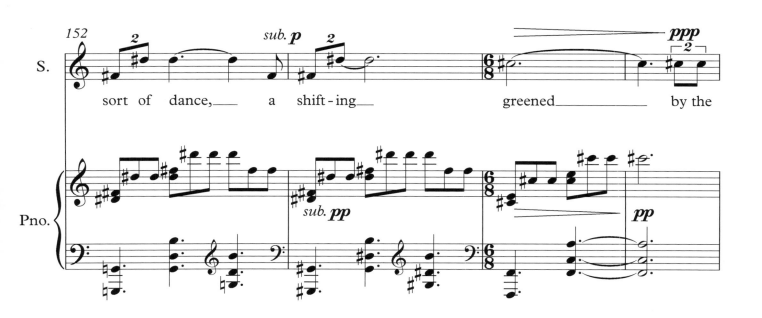

sort of dance,____ a shift-ing____ greened_____ by the

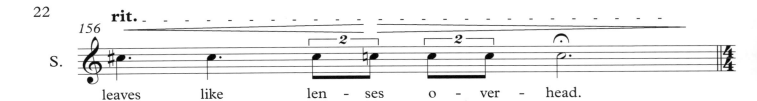

leaves like len-ses o-ver-head.

I think I named it after one of you, Claire's Sec-ret O-cean,

Zo-ë's Sec-ret Sea, far from the actual oceans you'd not seen yet.

Nei-ther of you knew___ that we were there to calm and change the

co - lor of my thought,_____ to ease its glaring pressure for a moment.

And we have been to-ge-ther o-ther pla- ces... for the same rea-son, which I can

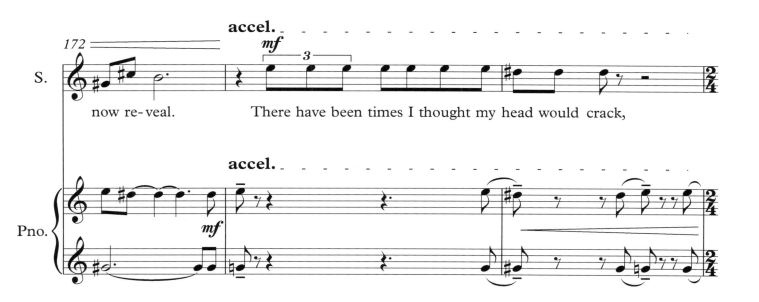

now re-veal. There have been times I thought my head would crack,

24

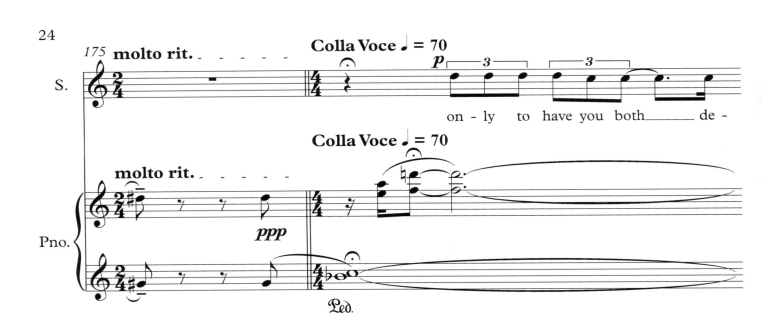

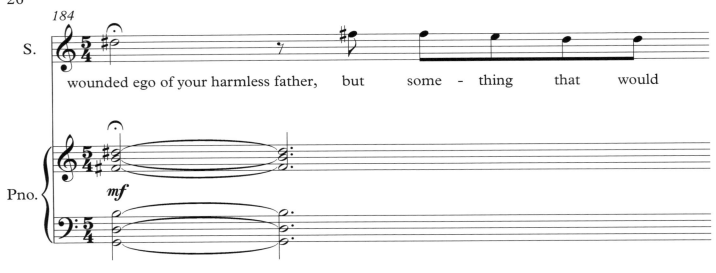

wounded ego of your harmless father, but some - thing that would

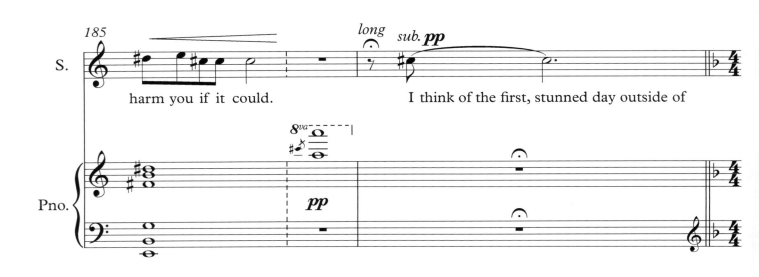

harm you if it could. I think of the first, stunned day outside of

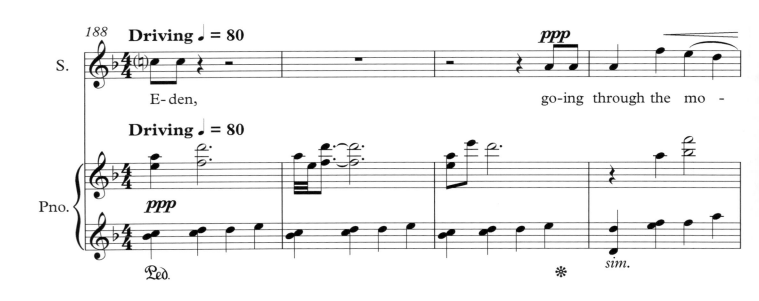

E - den, go-ing through the mo -

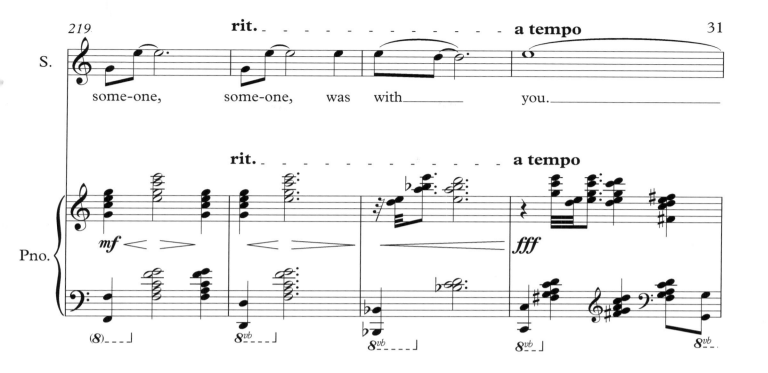

Made in the USA
Columbia, SC
28 November 2020